JESUS HEALS A MAN

NAME _____

GOSPEL
John 9:1-41

CODE MESSAGE

To find an important thing Jesus said in the Gospel story, write the correct letter under each number. The key will tell you which letter to write.

KEY

1 = A	8 = H	15 = O	22 = V
2 = B	9 = I	16 = P	23 = W
3 = C	10 = J	17 = Q	24 = X
4 = D	11 = K	18 = R	25 = Y
5 = E	12 = L	19 = S	26 = Z
6 = F	13 = M	20 = T	
7 = G	14 = N	21 = U	

9   1   13   20   8   5

12   9   7   8   20   15   6   20   8   5

23   15   18   12   4

SCRAMBLED WORDS

Unscramble these words from the Gospel story. Print them on the lines to the right. Then print the circled letters on the line below. Unscramble them to learn what the blind man did at the end of the story.

Jesus saw a man who had always been NIBDL.

Ⓞ _ _ _ _

Jesus made mud with earth and VASILA.

_ _ _ _ Ⓞ _

He put it on the man's YEES.

Ⓞ _ _ _

"Go wash in the POLO of Siloam," He said.

_ _ _ Ⓞ

Then the man could EES.

_ Ⓞ _

The SHARPIEES were upset.

_ _ _ _ Ⓞ _ _ _

But the man said, "He DONEEP my eyes."

_ _ Ⓞ _ _

_ _ _ _ _ _ _ _ _

SOMETHING TO DRAW

What do you think the blind man first saw when Jesus made him well? Draw it in the space below.

ANSWERS

CODE MESSAGE:

I am the light of the world.

SCRAMBLED WORDS:

blind, saliva, eyes, pool, see, Pharisees, opened—believe

JESUS FEEDS THOUSANDS

NAME _____

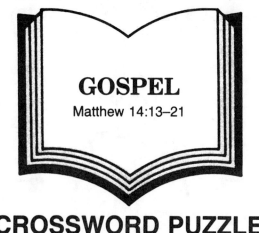

GOSPEL
Matthew 14:13–21

CROSSWORD PUZZLE

Try to fit words from the Gospel story into the crossword puzzle.(If you need help, use the wordlist.)

A (*1 across*) of people followed Jesus. He healed their (*2 down*). But (*3 across*) came and they needed (*4 down*). The disciples had only (*5 across*) loaves of (*6 down*) and two (*4 across*). Jesus told the people to (*2 across*) down. He (*7 down*) thanks and broke the loaves. Over five (*8 down*) got enough to eat!

WORD LIST:
THOUSAND
EVENING
CROWD
FISH
GAVE
FOOD
SICK
BREAD
SIT
FIVE

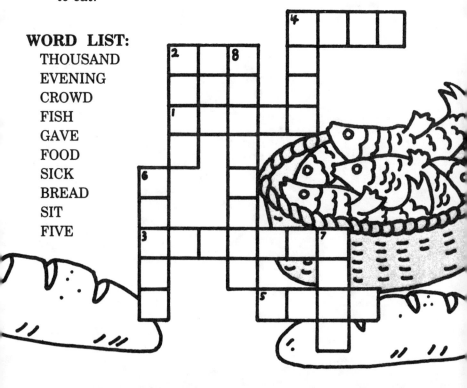

SOMETHING TO DRAW

Draw faces for the people below.

How did the sick people look before Jesus healed them?

How did the sick people look after Jesus healed them?

How did the disciples look when they knew the crowd was hungry?

How did the disciples look after Jesus fed the crowd?

HIDDEN NUMBER

The disciples filled baskets with *left-overs* after Jesus fed the crowd. To find out how many baskets they filled, color the spaces with dots.

ANSWERS

CROSSWORD PUZZLE:

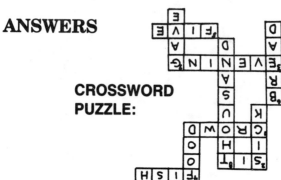

Printed in U.S.A.

JESUS HEALS 10 SICK MEN

NAME _____

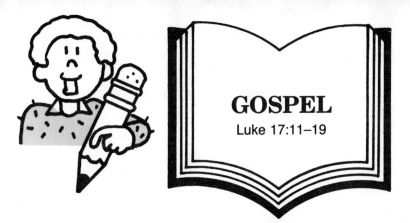

GOSPEL
Luke 17:11–19

CROSSWORD PUZZLE

Try to fit words from the Gospel story into the crossword puzzle. (If you need help, use the word list.)

Jesus was going to a (*1 down*). He met (*2 across*) men who had (*3 across*). They called, "Jesus, Master, have (*4 down*) on us!" Jesus told them to (*5 down*) themselves to the (*6 down*). He had (*7 down*) them! (*8 down*) came back. He (*9 across*) Jesus. Jesus asked, "Where are the other (*10 across*)?" Then He told the man to (*11 down*) and go.

WORD LIST:

PRIESTS PITY
SHOW   NINE
TEN   ONE
VILLAGE RISE
LEPROSY
THANKED
HEALED

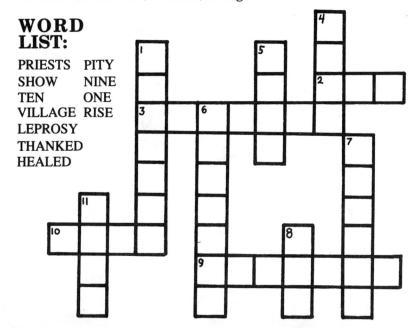

SOMETHING TO DRAW

Draw five things you can thank Jesus for.

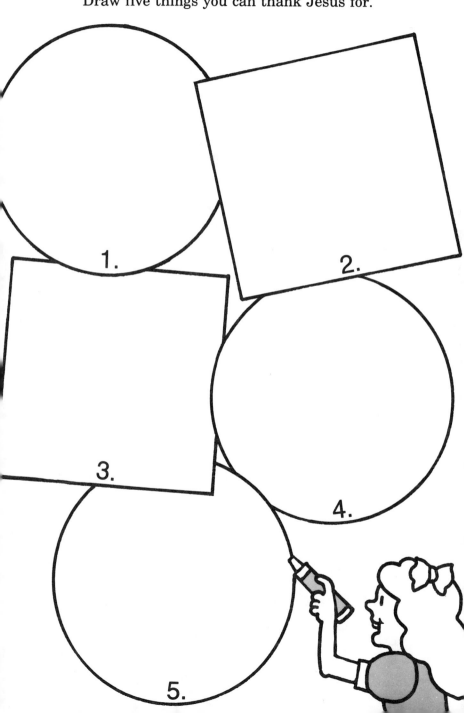

EMPTY SQUARES

See if you can fit Jesus' words into the squares below. One word has been done for you.

RISE AND GO; YOUR FAITH HAS MADE YOU WELL.

JESUS CALMS THE STORM

NAME _____

GOSPEL

Mark 4:35-41

WORD SEARCH

Try to find 12 words from the Gospel story in the puzzle. You may go up or down, from side to side, or diagonally. Circle each word as you find it and mark it off the list. The first one has been done for you.

CROWD
WAVES
WIND
CALM
BOAT
SLEEPING
QUIET
AFRAID
SQUALL
DROWN
STILL
FAITH

D	W	O	R	C	A	L	M
R	A	F	R	A	I	D	L
O	B	H	T	I	A	F	L
W	X	A	W	L	Y	Z	A
N	O	I	L	B	X	Y	U
B	N	I	T	E	I	U	Q
D	T	Z	W	A	V	E	S
S	L	E	E	P	I	N	G

SOMETHING TO DRAW

Here is a little boat. Can you draw a fierce storm around it?

Jesus is stronger than this storm too!

SOMETHING ELSE TO DRAW

In the space below, draw a picture of something that frightens *you*.

ANSWERS

WORD SEARCH:

Jesus is stronger than that too!

Printed in U.S.A.

JESUS RAISES A YOUNG GIRL

NAME _____

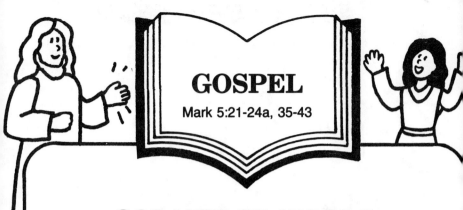

GOSPEL
Mark 5:21-24a, 35-43

SCRAMBLED WORDS

Unscramble these words from the Gospel story and print them on the lines at the right side. Then print the circled letters on the lines below. Unscramble them to learn what Jesus told the sick girl's father to do.

Jairus **LEFL** at Jesus' feet.

He said his little girl was **INDYG.**

If Jesus put His hands on her, she would **VEIL.**

Then some men told Jairus that his daughter was **ADDE.**

They said he shouldn't **TROBEH** Jesus anymore.

But Jesus **TWEN** with him anyway.

And Jesus made the **TILLET** girl well.

PICTURE PUZZLE

Jesus told the people to give that little girl something to eat. How many things to eat can you find hidden in this picture?

SOMETHING TO DRAW

In the space below, draw a picture of someone who helps you get well when you're sick.

JESUS, OUR GOOD SHEPHERD

NAME _____

GOSPEL
John 10:11-18

CROSSWORD PUZZLE

Try to fit words from the Gospel reading into the puzzle. (If you need help, use the word list.)

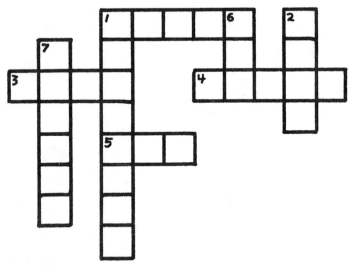

Jesus said He is the good (*1 down*). He lays (*2 down*) His (*3 across*) for the (*1 across*). He (*4 across*) His sheep and they know (*5 across*). He has sheep that are not of this sheep (*6 down*) too. They will also (*7 down*) to His voice.

WORD	DOWN	SHEPHERD	LISTEN	KNOWS
LIST:	SHEEP	LIFE	HIM	PEN

SOMETHING ✏ TO DRAW

How many sheep can you draw in this meadow? The good shepherd takes care of them all —and Jesus takes care of you.

Dot-to-Dot

Shepherds must protect their sheep. Connect th dots to see one thing th protect them from.

ANSWERS

CROSSWORD PUZZLE:

Printed in U.S.A.

JESUS BLESSES THE CHILDREN

NAME _____

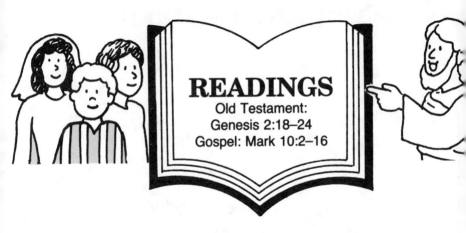

READINGS
Old Testament:
Genesis 2:18–24
Gospel: Mark 10:2–16

CROSSWORD PUZZLE

Try to fit words from the Gospel story into the crossword puzzle. (If you need help, use the word list.)

People brought little (*1 down*) to Jesus. The (*2 across*) scolded them. Jesus said, "Let the little children (*1 across*) to me." He took the children in his (*3 across*). Then he put his (*4 across*) on them and (*5 down*) them.

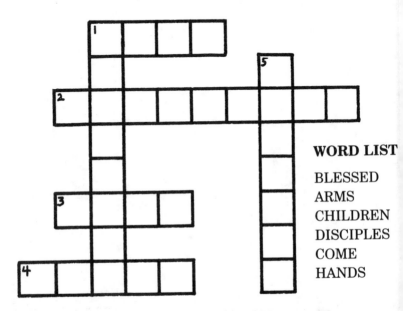

WORD LIST

BLESSED
ARMS
CHILDREN
DISCIPLES
COME
HANDS

HIDDEN ANIMALS

In the Old Testament story, Adam got to name the animals God had made. Can you help him find some of those animals? There are seven hiding in this picture.

SOMETHING TO DRAW

Today children come to Jesus in different ways. They pray. They worship Him in church. They read or hear stories about Him. They sing songs to Him. In the space below, draw a picture of yourself coming to Jesus.

ANSWERS

CROSSWORD PUZZLE:

JESUS CARES FOR EVEN THE SPARROWS

NAME _____

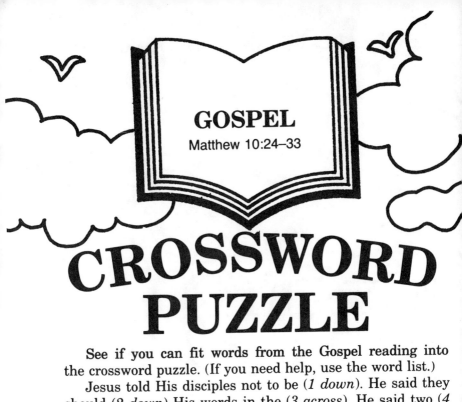

GOSPEL
Matthew 10:24–33

CROSSWORD PUZZLE

See if you can fit words from the Gospel reading into the crossword puzzle. (If you need help, use the word list.)

Jesus told His disciples not to be (*1 down*). He said they should (*2 down*) His words in the (*3 across*). He said two (*4 across*) are sold for a (*5 down*). But they won't (*6 across*) unless God lets them. He said, "And even the very (*7 down*) of your (*7 across*) are all numbered."

WORD LIST:

SPARROWS
AFRAID
DAYLIGHT
HAIRS
SPEAK
HEAD
PENNY
FALL

PICTURE PUZZLE

Jesus said that God cares about sparrows. But He cares about you even more. Can you find ten sparrows hidden in this picture?

SOMETHING TO DRAW

In the space below, draw a picture of something that frightens you. Then say a prayer. Ask God to protect you from that thing.

CROSSWORD PUZZLE:

ANSWER